M.S. Dhoni – The Legend's Playbook:

Leadership Handbook from the Master of the Craft

@9000RPM Publishing Works

Rajat Narang

ISBN:

Published by: Rajat Narang - 9000RPM Works

Cover Page Design: Canva.com

Cover Image: Dreamstime.com

Cover Image Credits: Mitchell Gunn | Image ID: 56976971

Back Cover Image: © Lakshmanan S (Latchu)

Also by the Authors:

Airbus vs. Boeing: Aviation's Dramatic Narrow-Body Cliffhanger Spanning 3+ Decades – Strategy Perspective – Part I & Part II - By Rajat Narang

Airbus vs. Boeing: Strategy Wars, Tactical Dogfights, High-G Maneuvers and the Photo Finishes – 1970s to 2020 – Rajat Narang

Birds of Fray – World's Top 4.5 & 5th Gen Fighter Jet Aircraft Programs

Birds of Fray: Top Gun Maverick: Special Edition

Phoenix Junction: The Cauldron of Inner Alchemy – By Bhumika Chandra

DEDICATED TO:

The Legend, MSD, himself for having inspired and continuing to inspire generations with his humility, simplicity, camaraderie and true leadership on and off the field…

Disclaimer

The Authors do not have any kind of financial investments, direct or indirect business associations or financial stakes of any sort in MSD or any of the companies or businesses owned, run or promoted by him. This work does not promote or endorse any particular individual, company or industry OEM & its products over others in any manner whatsoever.

The opinions expressed throughout are purely authors' personal and the views & judgments presented are neither directed or targeted at anyone nor meant as pontification of any sort and are solely based on objective assessment of the subject matter. The names of products, systems and/or brand names mentioned wherever through the work are intellectual property of their respective owners and their mention has been done only & purely for information & creative purposes and it does not indicate or reflect and should not be construed as any kind of endorsement or promotion of any kind. The authors do not have any direct business association with any of the mentioned leadership theorists, authors & other domain specialists of past or present and do not have any commercial stakes involved in any of their works or publications.

The work intends to provide a structural analysis of the leadership strategies, practices developed, cultivated & pursued by MSD on the field through his playing career, especially, from 2007-2016 period; which has been referred to as the prime span of reference for this work. The contents are not intended at chronicling his life, career events or glorification of achievements etc. in any broad or specific ways from a fan boy's perspective. The intent has been to provide objective analysis based on facts from the perspective of leadership against the light of some of the existing, most prominent leadership theories by some of the pre-eminent domain scholars while firmly toeing the thin line of objectivity right in the middle without getting awed by the fanfare or swayed by the criticism. The leadership context presented here has tactical leadership as the core pivot with focus on small, specialized & high performance teams.

The analysis has been purely anchored on informational evidences sourced from resources available in public domain with due citations and utmost effort has been made to ensure fair play to present the most objective view of reality in light of the available facts & evidences rather than taking a biased view. The approach taken, thus, is intended to provide a collection of clear principles pertaining to leadership followed by & derived from M.S. Dhoni's on-field play, media interviews by MSD himself & other cricket players and structured as a handbook.

All the information, data & facts presented herein have been derived from reliable secondary sources, reasonably verified & have been presented for informational purposes only All effort & due diligence has been done to ensure the accuracy of the same, however, the same can't be guaranteed. The views & opinions expressed throughout have been presented in light of the supporting facts & evidences by duly citing the sources alongside. Feel free to write in case of any concerns. The relevant jurisdiction in case of any judicial intervention would solely be New Delhi.

The presented content contains generic information only and is not suitable for addressing specific or particular circumstances of any specific case or scenario. The content, thus, is not intended to be used as a basis for taking decisions of commercial or any other nature. The authors and the publisher disclaim all liabilities originating from the outcomes of the application of the contents in real-life scenarios without duly conducting thorough due diligence and without seeking professional advice & opinion from relevant subject matter experts.

Introduction

Leadership and MSD have more or less become synonymous with each other given the legend's unparalleled display of the same over the past 2 decades. This handbook, therefore, intends to derive the key principles & best practice pertaining to the leadership domain from MSD himself and his on-field application of them which have brought him immense success. The intent is to create a sort of handbook or best practices guide which could be a quick to go through while being a useful and readily applicable guiding beacon across domains for the present and the generations yet to come.

The handbook, thus, has not been tightly structured and derives from information available in the public domain sources using secondary research.

1.

Focus on Inputs & Controllables, i.e., Process & Efforts rather than Outcomes

The core pivot of MSD's approach to the game has forever been the focus on inputs, efforts and the parameters that can be controlled rather than the outcomes. It emanates from his stoic personality which limits the degree of impact emotions and outside forces & noises have on his headspace which enables him to stay calm and composed in some of the most turbulent situations at critical junctures of the game on the field. This remarkable ability of him is what has effectively made him earn the well deserved moniker of 'Captain Cool'. It is this approach which has enabled him to take calculated risks and chances without bothering about the outcomes of the decisions.

That's what's behind MSD's usual stoic, Spartan way of celebrating even after winning major tournaments, as he realizes that it is not just about those moments but rather about the culmination of long journeys, and, thus, his minimalistic personal approach to the degree of emotional expression. This complete and intense focus on efforts takes away the pressure of outcomes off his head and shoulders while facing crunch situations with immense ease and enables him to give his 100% in any given moment and ensures that he is able to deliver the goods most of the times.

As the legend himself has said, "Worry about the controllables. Thinking about the results will not give you the results. Taking care of small steps helps" – MSD

2.

100% Effort = Victory

With the team ethos and culture fabricated around inputs and efforts rather than outcomes, failure as an outcome is fully acceptable but not giving one's 100% at all times is not…When the pressure of outcomes is not there as the hanging sword ready to strike, the players and the team do not feel jittery and play with intensity while fully enjoying the game and expressing themselves on the field completely in an uninhibited manner as failure is a perfectly acceptable part of the process but flinching & shirking away from giving one's hundred percent always under all circumstances is not. Winning becomes a habit and comes naturally to everyone at the conscious as well as sub-conscious level and even the big matches as well as tournament finals seem devoid of pressure & any major variation in mercury levels.

This is the culture and ethos of the Chennai Super Kings (CSK) cricket team & franchise in a nutshell, wherein, under MSD, CSK has been able to become one of the most successful teams in the Indian Premier League (IPL) having won the title four times. Many former & current CSK players have ratified in media interviews as to how the players don't have any pressure of expectations or winning on them from the management or the franchise.

The skipper MSD himself remarked after CSK's relatively poor showing in IPL 2022, owing to an attempted leadership transition, after a win in the IPL 2021. He said, following CSK's comprehensive win against Delhi Capitals, ""If we make the playoffs, great. But even if we don't it's not the end of the world. I am not a big fan of maths. Even in school, I wasn't good at it. Thinking of the net run-rate doesn't help. You just want to enjoy the IPL. When two other teams are playing, you don't want to be under pressure and thinking. You just have to think about what to do in the next game."[4]

In an interview given to ESPN Cricinfo after India's win in the T20 World Cup of 2007, Dhoni outlined his philosophy in exact same words, "I believe in giving more than 100% on the field and I don't really worry about the result if there's great commitment on the field. That's victory for me."[9]

xiv

3.

TAKING FULL & COMPLETE OWNERSHIP

The 2020 season of the IPL, played in the UAE amid pandemic woes in India was one of the worst seasons for CSK with the team clearly struggling throughout the tournament and finishing at the second last position on the points table for the first time ever losing 8 matches of the 14 total matches it played. MSD, however, in post match presentations, accepted complete ownership & responsibility for the team's dismal performances as the skipper following availability of limited practice opportunities prior to the tournament owing to COVID-19 related series of lockdowns & restrictions.

When CSK lost three matches in a row in the tournament, he said in the post match presentation, "Long time back since we lost three in a row. We need to get a lot of things right. It is the professionalism. We need to take our catches & not bowl no-balls. Those are the controllables and may-be we are getting too relaxed".[1]

Regarding his own performance with the bat, he was forthright in accepting, "I was not able to middle a lot of deliveries. Was trying to hit it too hard. When the wicket is slightly at the slower side, it is better to time it. Looking at outfield it was subconsciously coming to us to hit the ball hard,"[1]

When a leader exercises complete & extreme ownership, irrespective of the fallout, it instills a sense of immense personal responsibility & accountability through the rank & file with everyone guided by that internal moral compass. When that happens, it creates a culture of constant improvement, high performance & betterment which accepts failures as an integral part of the process, instead of a culture of blame-game & finding scapegoats, which is simply disastrous, as it hinders the process of learning & improvement.

Another example of extreme ownership in action from MSD came in the just abandoned IPL 2021 in India. When the players were to check out & depart from the team hotel following the suspension of the marquee event, MSD declared to the CSK team management, like the true captain of the ship in the popular tradition of the sea, that he would be the last one to leave the team hotel after CSK players get home safe. "Mahi bhai said that he will be the last person to leave the hotel. He wanted foreigners to leave first, then the Indian players. He will be taking the last flight tomorrow when everyone reaches their home safe and secure,"[2] as quoted by one of the CSK team members to the Indian Express.

4.

Team First: "Rather than Focusing on Your Score, Focus on What Your Team Requires"

Former Indian skipper, Virat Kohli, had the following to say about MSD while speaking to media prior to 2019's ODI World Cup. He said, "There's one thing about MS that's far more important than anything else - and there's a lot to him - for him, the team is always above everything else. It's always about the team, no matter what."[3]

When Hardik Pandya was asked by Dinesh Karthik (after the former's super performance for Gujrat Titans in IPL 2022) in a one-to-one as to how does he manage to stay calm and handle pressure so well; Hardik revealed another Brahmastra (super weapon) given to him by MSD. He said MS told him to focus on what the team requires in any given situation rather than focusing on his own score. Focusing on his score or the current reality would only cause worry and create pressure, whereas, focusing on the team's need would give him a tangible goal to focus upon and make him achieve it given that the human brain truly is an incredible goal seeking system. Those who have read the wonderful book, Psychocybernetics, a timeless classic from Dr. Maxwell Maltz, would instantly attest to that.

Further, focusing on a superordinate goal, like team's need, gives a player extra motivation & drive to achieve it rather than a personal goal. Also, when every player keeps the team above everything else, it automatically leads to team cohesion and every player giving more than his 100% to the team's cause.

5.

"ANYTHING IS ALWAYS POSSIBLE" – MSD

All of us have been a witness to the Mahi magic since his advent to international cricket in 2004 and his tremendous self-belief and remarkable ability to change the fate of any game at any given juncture single handedly, like a precise mission with his surgical strikes without even a trace of emotion, be it the 2011 ODI World Cup win or the victory in ICC's Champions Trophy in 2013.

This characteristic calmness, undying self-belief & optimism and never-say-attitude from the leader to be able to change the outcome has imbued & forged the same grit & fighting spirit in his team mates and Indian cricket's DNA over the years.

This is what Captain Pete Mitchell, aka, Maverick also does as the leader of the pack in the latest Paramount movie and sequel to the 1986's original blockbuster, Top Gun: Maverick, wherein, he is required to train a group of elite U.S. Navy fighter pilots for a daring & challenging mission. However, mid-way during the training the pilots are seen to be giving up on the very belief in the mission's achievability in the given time frame. Maverick, then, effectively demonstrates by undertaking and successfully simulating the mission characteristics in even lesser time than actually stipulated for the mission with his skillful aerial flying and aerobatic maneuvers which restores & instills their self-belief in the feasibility of the mission.

This is exactly what MSD has done to the Indian team and Indian Cricket over the years with his sheer presence, skills and self-belief…

6.

Leadership 'Presence' rather than just 'Charisma' with focus on 'Authenticity'

Charisma is characterized by intense, focused emotion which shows up in the body language first and then in the actual message of someone exhibiting it. Charismatic leaders are simply authentic and thus, invariably have a perfect alignment between their body language and their message to the followers, thereby, producing charisma[5,6]

Another related but different and more holistic concept is 'Leadership Presence' based on the "Three Levels of Leadership Model" developed by James Scouller and published in his titular book in 2011. Presence contrastingly also includes the leader's psychology, degree of personal self-mastery, authenticity and an attitude of service towards followers as the core tenets. Scouller has differentiated effectively between Charisma and Presence and has argued that "leaders can be charismatic by relying on a job title, fame, skillful acting or by the projection of an aura of "specialness" by followers – whereas presence is something deeper, more authentic, more fundamental and more powerful and does not depend on social status"[7]

Scouller has further defined Presence as follows, "At its root, it is wholeness – the rare but attainable inner alignment of self-identity, purpose and feelings that eventually leads to freedom from fear. It reveals itself as the magnetic, radiating effect you have on others when you're being the authentic you, giving them your full respect and attention, speaking honestly and letting your unique character traits flow. As leaders, we must be technically competent to gain others' respect, but it's our unique genuine presence that inspires people and prompts them to trust us – in short, to want us as their leader."[7] The two, however, are not mutually exclusive as there have been exceptional leaders who have exercised both charisma as well as presence in an integrative manner.

Kirsten had the following to say about Dhoni at the end of his 3 year tenure as the coach of Indian team. He said, "One word that comes to my mind about Dhoni's leadership is presence. I put the words — inspiration and presence —

together, because I believe, I was in a position to inspire people through my work ethic whereas Dhoni was a leader for them through presence. He has this X-factor and walks around with his presence." He further added, "Winning and losing don't mean a lot to him, he just gets on with it. He has this uncanny presence about him without saying much. People want to follow him, people want to go with him. I want to go to war with this guy"[8]

7.

"The One Who Panics Last Wins the Game" – MSD

The area where MSD had the maximum impact upon his advent to the Indian cricket team at the international level was the ability to not choke in high pressure situations and knockout games like the semi-finals & finals of major international ICC tournaments. India's capitulation or rather Australia's absolute dominance of the Indian cricket team, led by an unstoppable Ricky Ponting, in the 2003's ODI World Cup final in Johannesburg is still a painful memory for Indian cricket and the fans. However, all of that changed with a flamboyant Dhoni who would, leveraging his strengths of holding the nerve and his big hitting ability, would take the pressure games to the very end towards nail-biting finishes while putting opposition under the pump. And once there, he would hammer, outplay & outclass them with his power, range of orthodox & unconventional shots and stroke play.

This was the operating model with which he led India to victory in the ICC's maiden T20 World Cup held in South Africa in 2007 while caring a damn about the traditional, high-pressure India-Pakistan rivalry in the final of the world cup. Dhoni and his band of rookies held their nerve while defending a small total and clinched the game on the very last ball of the match. In 2011's ODI World Cup final, too, Dhoni came to the fore with India chasing a big total made by Sri Lanka and in his typical manner; he simply iced the game and took it away from the Sri Lankans. The same story repeated itself in the 2013's rain afflicted Champions Trophy final in England where India successfully defended a small total of 129 while defying the rain gods.

Dhoni's this remarkable quality was a clear outlier and gave him a definite competitive advantage and edge over opponents for a significantly long span of time till the proliferation of T20 as the most popular & dominant format in the game of cricket which made temperament, pressure handling and holding nerves as a critical & indispensable part of the game as chasing 50-60 runs in the last 5 overs became achievable and almost norm of the day. **F-16E/F:** E was single seat variant while F was twin seat variant. The E/F featured an advanced AESA radar, advanced Avionics, Conformal Fuel Tanks (CFTs) and higher thrust GE engine, namely, F110-GE-132 engine.

8.

"God will not come Down to Help Us, Fight it Out Yourself…"- MSD

The mighty statement and piece of advice was rendered by none other than MSD at the 2013's Champions Trophy final wherein India were defending a paltry total of 129 in a rain affected match which effectively became a T20 game rather than an ODI game, as originally scheduled, as it had to be reduced from 50 overs to 20 overs per side owing to loss of playing time due to rain. While defending, India started off well having decimated England's top order by having taken 4 wickets for 46 runs by the 9th over. However, following a 64-run partnership between Eoin Morgan and Ravi Bopara for the 5th wicket, England were comfortably placed at 110 runs for 4 wickets by 17.2 overs as they needed just 20 more runs to win off 16 balls. At that juncture, the Indian team looked almost clueless as the game and the trophy both were slipping out of their hands.

At that moment, the skipper MS Dhoni, looking to buck up and inspire his troops, uttered these words which have become as popular as he himself is and are still quoted. The team was all charged and fired up following Dhoni's command and they wrapped up the game on the last ball of the match with a wicket with England still short of the target by 6 runs despite having 2 wickets in hand.

After the match, MSD unraveled in the post match presentation as to how the tactical decision to bring in Ishant Sharma to bowl the 18th over turned the game around on its head as the windy conditions were helping Ishant's seam & pace and he made the most of it by getting the wickets of Eoin Morgan and Ravi Bopara off consecutive balls, with both the catches taken by Ravichandran Ashwin, which brought the English tail to the fore and thus, effectively unlocked the door to India's maiden Champions Trophy win.

9.

Success Breeds more Success by Instilling a Habit of Winning

This is what Dhoni had to say after India's win in the 2007's inaugural ICC Twenty20 World Cup as the leader of the pack in a media interview. MSD said while elaborating in a candid media interview given to ESPN Cricinfo just 6 months after winning the T20 world cup in 2007 as to how winning that cup propelled the team on to the pathway & habit of winning. He said, "In the Twenty20 World Cup we were thirsty. We tasted victory and we knew how it feels to be victorious. That really worked for us. The World Twenty20 win was the starting point - not from the victory point of view but the way we performed, the way we enjoyed each other's success. Even some of the senior guys who'd missed out, their involvement was great. Everybody was coming up with ideas; everybody wanted to win each and every game. That was the turning point. After that we started enjoying each other's success.

If I score a hundred, of course I will enjoy it. But if your team-mates start enjoying your hundred that's when you know you are moving in the right direction. That's what is needed"[2]

The initial set of successes further build up temperament where the players and the team do not feel jittery and play with intensity while fully enjoying the game without pressure of expectations or outcome as failure is a perfectly acceptable part of the process but

flinching & shirking away from giving one's hundred percent always under all circumstances is not. Winning becomes a habit and comes naturally to everyone at the conscious as well as sub-conscious level and even the big matches as well as tournament finals seem devoid of pressure & any major variation in mercury levels.

When a team continuously & constantly seeks improvement & perfection, after a while it becomes an innate part of the team culture, a sub-conscious habit at the individual as well as collective level, something which also alters the team DNA in the process, programming it for an eternal quest for improvements & success. After all, success breeds success.

10.

Ability to Mentor & Coach Rookies Effectively

The ability to induct, mentor & coach rookies & newcomers into the team effectively and helping them learn the ropes without them feeling alienated, bullied or commanded requires sensitivity from the leader at the helm and a healthy team culture. The IPL teams which have done it most successfully over the years have obviously been CSK and the Mumbai Indians with MSD's natural knack for grooming talent having turned CSK almost into a MSD finishing academy for cricket.

The same had been most evident and on display in the IPL 2022, wherein, playing without their ace pace bowler and core pivot of their strike force, Deepak Chahar, who could not play due to an injury, CSK clearly lacked firepower and had to deploy its string of uncapped pace bowlers as the spearhead of their pace attack and their relative inexperience was evident on-field.

However, MSD's active mentoring and precise tactical guidance from behind the stumps along with the efforts by CSK's bowling coaches throughout the tournament had such an effect that by the fag end of the tournament they looked like an entirely different species, especially, Mukesh Choudhary, who was swinging the ball beautifully with full control and somehow made up for Deepak Chahar absence to some extent.

Mukesh Choudhary and Simarjeet Singh together put up an excellent display of pace bowling in the match against Mumbai Indians where the duo together bowled the opening 8 overs of the game and reduced Mumbai to 33/4.

MS Dhoni had the following to say about the duo in his post match presentation, "Irrespective of how the wicket is, anything below 130 is very difficult to defend, but still, what I asked the bowlers was to show a lot of character, put the opposition under pressure, forget about the result, and I feel both the youngsters, both the fast bowlers, they bowled really well,"[10] He further added, "So as far as their contribution is concerned, I feel a game like this really helps them. They start believing in themselves by saying, okay, irrespective of the conditions, whenever we start, we need to have the same kind of attitude, and that's what is needed in the shortest format"[10]

Former Indian Cricketer turned commentator, Aakash Chopra, had the following to say about M.S. Dhoni's grooming of Mukesh Choudhary, ""If anyone bowls the best with the new ball, I feel it is Mukesh Choudhary. We saw him bowling at the death also where he used the natural angle of taking it across, which all left-armers do. Captain Dhoni slowly-slowly got him to bowl at the death as well."[11] He further added, " This is captain Dhoni's plan - he first gets you to bowl more with the new ball and then prepares you slowly, then finishes you in the 14th or 15th over and then gives you the 19th or 20th over as well. He stood out in every challenge."[11]

Mukesh Choudhary told media in an interview, following CSK's match against SRH when asked about what Dhoni had told him, ""He just told me to bowl normally and even though I tried a couple of different deliveries, he just said bowl normally as they require a lot of runs. So just bowl normally and 'Don't give a no-ball." [12]

MSD further commented in the post match presentation of the CSK's match against SRH wherein CSK were defending a total of 203, "I always told my bowlers, you may get hit for four sixes in an over, but the two balls that you save – ultimately in a high-scoring game – those are the two deliveries that will help you win the game. Because a lot of bowlers, after getting 3-4 sixes, they will be like let's get done with it but that one boundary or even instead of sixes if you get hit for two fours that will help you in a game. I don't know if they believe in that theory, but it works,"[13]

11.

Fingerspitzengefühl & Domain Leadership

Domain leadership, in contrast from the traditional connotation of leadership, i.e. people leadership, stands for specialists who have expertise in a particular domain. They use that domain authority to influence & help others, for anything across the board, having to do with that domain. Domain leadership, thus, enables the leader to tactically assess the situation extraordinarily and take the best call in the given, on-field scenario.

What these stalwarts of the domain tend to develop is a snap mental calculation or what is also called is a fingertip feel or 'Fingerspitzengefühl', in the German lexicon where it originated, with the term standing for 'intuitive flair' or 'instinct' or 'one's finger on the pulse'. Additionally, it also entails great situational awareness along with situational management with the ability to respond most appropriately & tactfully in a given situation. MSD, in fact, has talked very often about him being a pure instinct player & captain not believing & relying much on stats or theories.

This Fingerspitzengefühl is what guides MSD whether to take DRS calls or not in high pressure situations apart from the seemingly outlandish calls taken on the spur of the moment on multiple occasions, like giving the ball to Joginder Singh in 2007's Twenty20 tournament's final or his decision to bat himself up the order in 2011's ODI World Cup final, both of which ultimately turned out his way.

Even MSD himself says that his gut feeling is based on his past & vast experience. In an interview given to bcci.tv given in 2014 he had said, "I don't plan a lot and believe in my gut feel. But what many people don't understand is that to have that gut feel, you have to have experienced that thing before. My gut feeling comes from my past experiences of all the cricket I've played in my life and the situations I have faced. It's not something you just feel for a moment without any logic."[14]

12.

Domain Leadership, Natural Authority & Mentorship

What these extraordinary achievers or domain leaders also bring with them in their respective domains is an unparalleled, natural authority & respect as leaders, which makes them clearly stand a class apart, like a lighthouse with the guiding beacon, which naturally brings respect to them in the leadership role.

This is what has brought him respect even from the opposition players. As transformational leaders, they inspire & motivate their followers to consistently pursue excellence, outperform and go beyond their limitations while following & fulfilling their internal sense of purpose. They also help & enable their followers in consistently upping their game by a notch or two to a further higher orbit by guiding them with their experience & wisdom while providing the much needed directional course & nudge.

MSD has been a natural at mentoring & coaching young players as we all have seen over the years. For MSD, this list includes the bigwigs of India's present cricket line-up, including, Virat Kohli, Rohit Sharma, Ravindra Jadeja, Hardik Pandya and the spinning duo of Kuldeep & Chahal; at some point or the other of their playing careers. Also, his mentoring & coaching initiatives have not just remained restricted to the men he commanded on-field in the national cricket team or the CSK. He has often been seen even mentoring young players from other teams in the IPLs as well.

The extraordinary domain competence, thus, enables the leader to mentor & shape his troops effectively while the special, personal connect he develops in the process enables him to marshal & inspire his troops to go above & beyond the call of duty on the battlefield and bridge that gap between the ordinary and the extraordinary.

13.

Humility and Humble Leadership – Focus on Followers rather than Self

The focus of the leader should not be on himself as the captain of the ship but rather on the followers with the relationships shaped by transparent communication, openness, trust & empathy which naturally come from humility; instead of hierarchy & power distance; the hallmarks of traditional & the conventional concept of leadership. Humility also enables the leader to focus on his own shortcomings and keep evolving as a person as well as leader.

Humble leaders, as leaders, thus, focus on the development of their followers as well, in the process, rather than treating them as just the means to get to end results. This creates a culture of trust, openness, relationship, camaraderie & mutual respect shaped by transparent & open communication. This interpersonal culture of transparency &

communication, in combination with the culture of extreme ownership, under a leader exercising transformational leadership, to inspire his team to chase challenging goals, leads to extraordinary results in myriad ways.

14.

Exercising Transformational Leadership – Inspiring Troops to Go Above & Beyond the Call of Duty

The concept of Transforming leadership was first referred to by James MacGregor Burns in 1978 who took the concept of leadership beyond its traditional roots anchored in the transactional approach. He described it as a "process in which leaders & followers help each other to advance to a higher level of morale & motivation" [15]. Bernard M. Bass18 evolved it into 'Transformational Leadership' by taking the concept a step further and elaborating it based on underlying psychological mechanisms at play.

He explains that "transformation is at play when a transformational leader inspires & elevates his followers to go beyond their own self-interests to work towards the collective good and the team's success based on a mutually shared vision." [16] The leader with charisma develops a personal, special emotional connect with his followers based on individualized consideration by addressing their respective individual concerns & needs through coaching & mentoring etc.

Further, with his idealized influence, he inspires & stirs them up emotionally to take up challenges and go way above & beyond the line of duty for the team & the mission. The transformational leader, thus, gains respect & trust, instills a sense of pride in the team & leads as a role model with the followers looking up to him for inspiration with faith, respect & confidence. He gives them purpose, meaningful & challenging goals and in a way addresses their self-expression & self-actualization need, as outlined in the Maslow's hierarchy of needs theory of motivation.

Transformational leadership has been the traditional backbone of military leadership as the team collectively faces high stakes, extraordinary situations, involving precious human lives, on a daily basis. A wrong call, in what are literally life & death situations, could seal the fate of many in a matter of minutes & seconds. That's what has driven soldiers to even dive over enemy grenades in combat zones in order to save their comrades from a certain death and not letting them & the team down come what may. There have been countless stories, transcending the borders of time and space, of extraordinarily brave soldiers staking & even losing their lives for their mates and for a cause larger than them.

15.

Creating Autonomous, Self-Directed Teams

When a leader exercises Transformational Leadership, what he creates in the process, is a culture of high performance, strong goal-orientation & purpose-driven achievement and extreme ownership at the individual as well as collective level. This further creates highly motivated, skilled and self-directed teams capable of operating autonomously to take on any mission or task either with or without the leader.

They are based on decentralized organization principle and are also called self-directed teams working along a set of pre-defined objectives autonomously. In these specialized teams, the traditional hierarchy based command structures give way to flat, collaborative approaches which provide tremendous operational flexibility, resourcefulness & contingencies to navigate through murky waters & dark zones entailing unpredictable courses & potentially hazardous situations.

However, when a team continuously & constantly seeks improvement & perfection, after a while it becomes an innate part of the team culture, a sub-conscious habit at the individual as well as collective level, something which also alters the team DNA in the process, programming it for an eternal quest for improvement & success. After all, success breeds success. The initial set of successes further build up temperament where the players and the team do not feel jittery and play with intensity while fully enjoying the game without pressure of expectations or outcome as failure is a perfectly acceptable part of the process but flinching & shirking away from giving one's hundred percent always under all circumstances is not. Winning becomes a habit and comes naturally to everyone at the conscious as well as sub-conscious level and even the big matches as well as tournament finals seem devoid of pressure & any major variation in mercury levels.

Before Sourav Ganguly and MSD's advent to Indian Cricket, the team was prone to choking down in pressure situations with India-Pakistan cricket matches having been the prime example of the same. However, Dada inspired the team to never back down and fight back and galvanized his troops with resilience while MSD took the process to the next level with his nerves of steel. He demonstrated, while leading effectively by example, as to how to take the game to the wire and excel in crunch situations by putting pressure on the opponents. MSD also created the method or the process and set the winning template for the team which became a process and the team could do the same and win even without him which was proved following the rise of Virat Kohli as the captain as the team has continued to pursue excellence even in the post Virat Kohli era.

16.

Harnessing the Power of Super-Ordinate Goals

'Super' etymologically means above the ordinary, from Latin 'Supra' meaning 'above, over or beyond'. Super-ordinate goals, thus, literally are goals which are above or beyond ordinary goals. Super-ordinate goals, in the verbiage of goal-setting, are goals which provide meaning & purpose to an individual, team or an organization by being their very raison d'etre. How are these super-ordinate goals so effective and what is the mechanism by which they work? That's essentially the domain of neuroscience with the lead & pivotal role held by a neurotransmitter within our brain, known as Dopamine, as mentioned earlier as well.

Dopamine, as an essential element of the brain's neurochemistry, performs a myriad of functions in the human body. However, from the perspective of motivation & performance, what it does is make a situation, goal or task feel salient & meaningful to us and provides the motivation to work towards achieving the same. It happens with the release of Dopamine into specific areas of our brains, which, in addition to providing motivation, essentially also signals feedback for predicted & anticipated rewards likely to come our way from the achievement of the goal and it does it as a mechanism.

Thus, for a player, from the neuroscience perspective, the goal of playing a match winning inning for the team to take it to victory is much more salient, meaningful & fulfilling for the brain than a selfish goal of making a century for himself and being named as the player of the match. That's how the human brain is wired and it works the same way for altruism & pro-social behavior, wherein, helping others provides a similar sense of joy & satisfaction. Also, it is not restricted to just humans with even animals showing elements of altruistic behavior.

That's the phenomenon which used to be at work when we used to see Virat Kohli batting almost like a possessed man while chasing targets with the goal of getting team India to victory, especially in close or crucial matches. That is what also explains his incredible surge in batting averages while chasing targets, as against his career average, which literally goes into a super gear. Same goes for his batting average, which witnesses a major spike, while playing overseas as against home conditions. The more challenging it is treated by the brain, greater the motivation & the drive to perform and achieve with the body & mind operating in tandem in the overdrive mode

In the Indian cricket's context, the ODI World Cup of 2011 was a special occasion for two reasons. First, it was being held in India and second, it was the last world cup for the cricket legend, Sachin Tendulkar, who had been holding the reins of Indian cricket for over 2 decades. The Indian players, led by MSD, wanted to give a befitting farewell to their super hero whom they had idolized as children seeing him on the television while growing up. The team wanted to be the first one ever to win it on home soil and give the World Cup itself as the souvenir and almost a parting gift to the little master. They worked for it through the tournament and took Indian cricket to its second ODI world cup win after 28 years.

That's the power of the super-ordinate goal. In a clash of 'who wants it more' between the two teams on the field, it often boils down to the 'comparative strengths of the respective causes' they are battling it out for and most often victory favours the team with the relatively stronger & ideologically superior cause on a given day.

17.

ADAPTING & EVOLVING ONE'S GAME INCREMENTALLY

In the Cricketing realm, when a rookie Dhoni was looking to make it to the big league, his unconventional technique, too, was derided at by the experts of the game. While appearing for a selection for the Railway's Ranji Trophy team, way back in 2002, he was rejected after keeping wickets for just 3 balls, with the selectors simply unimpressed by his keeping as well as batting, finding him technically not sound enough to represent the Railways cricket team.

Even when he had made his way to the national team, the wicket-keeping experts of the yore, found his unconventional technique behind stumps to be unsound, with the former Indian wicket-keeper, Syed Kirmani, leading the pack. He has commented on it in media interviews, as recently as 2018, saying "If you talk about collection of the throw. He has to go right behind the stumps, not what Dhoni does (sometimes he takes it from ahead of stumps). [Rishabh] Pant is following him. It is not a technique. You have to get behind in line with the stumps; your eye level should be in line with the bails to see where the ball is pitching so that you can judge it better"[17]. He further said, "MS Dhoni's wicket-keeping style should not be aped by youngsters."[17] However, Dhoni worked on his game & effectively proved it otherwise with his on-field results & impact, both behind as well as in front of the stumps.

Dhoni started out as an explosive wicket-keeper batsman, who could turn the fat of the game with his bat in just a couple of overs, at any given juncture of the game. He was a maverick with the bat as well, with an unconventional technique, comprising a playbook of unorthodox shots, with the hallmark of the same being the helicopter shot, which he has used to great effect through his career.

However, he also evolved his game by transforming himself effectively from being the swashbuckler, mustang; who could also keep wickets, to the mature, wicket-keeper Captain Cool; seen today with his on-field presence, as the keeper and the captain, becoming the core of his game while batting has become relegated to a secondary role over the years.

That kind of evolution was necessary for him, from an evolutionary & longevity perspective, given that wicket-keeping is a tedious & laborious job requiring tremendous amount of focus, concentration & energy on every single ball. Thus, managing to think on one's feet, as the captain, on a sustained basis, along-with keeping wickets, is simply a herculean and a monumental task in itself.

This is what Virat Kohli had to say about his personal transition & the journey chasing excellence in a media interview given in May 2019, "Soon after 2012. That's the year when the transition began. It began more with the idea of inculcating a stricter sense of discipline and need for fitness. When I started my own transition in fitness the simple realization was that if I don't keep up with the demands of the game, I'm going to be an average cricketer. People will remember me as someone who did well for three or four years and then, kind of, was one among the many. I knew that I had to change everything about my life, about myself, to be able to be at the top of my game, to be in sync where the world (of sport) is heading." [18]

Talking about evolution & improvisation, both Virat Kohli and Sachin Tendulkar, kept evolving & improvising their game, as batsmen, through the incorporation of small, tactical changes & improvements throughout, including the addition of some new shots to their already vast arsenal of shots, which effectively limited the ability of the bowlers to study their respective games as a static construct & exploit weaknesses.

They remained dynamic, kept learning & evolving their game throughout and that's what made them so effective & successful.

Similarly, Harbhajan Singh's creation of Doosra and R. Ashwin's conception of the Carrom ball; effectively expanded their variations, took their game to a different level and eventually proved critical in their career successes. Similarly, Suresh Raina and Gautam Gambhir's perceived weaknesses & limitations against short bowling became well known and were exploited effectively by the bowlers against them.

As Bruce Lee has said, in sports as well as in life, the opponents will study your game looking to expose your weaknesses & exploit them and it happens eventually to everyone. However, the masters keep working on themselves and eventually turn their weaknesses into strengths with their perseverance, discipline & determination and that is what makes them extraordinary & ultimately sets them apart from the ordinary.

Thus, the only real competition one has is with oneself, with focus on realizing true potential, by becoming a better version of one's own self by growing incrementally with time.

18.

Being the Pioneer & Trailblazer – Rise of the Wicket-Keeper Batsman & Captain in Cricket following MSD

From a strategy perspective, the wicket-keeper's position is kind of a vantage point which provides the best possible positioning on the field to monitor, observe & control the game most effectively, if one is able to manage & sustain the additional workload that comes along with it. That is why we haven't really seen many wicket-keeper captains in the game historically.

MSD has been one of the first and most successful wicket-keeper batsmen India has ever produced. He pioneered the concept of wicket-keeper captain and an explosive batsman down the batting order who could finish the game with his muscle power. He created a unique positioning for himself strategically, being a true trailblazer, which had unmatched value proposition for the team. MSD's success proved the value of the template which has become really popular, especially, in the IPLs.

The emergence of wicket-keeping captains in cricket, has been explored in a recent article, appearing in 'The Hindu', which sought views from the English wicket-keeper batsman, Jos Buttler, Englands wicket-keeper batsman, about the growing trend. Butler concurs with the view, that a wicket-keeper indeed gets the best, 360 degree view of the game with his tremendous positional advantage and this provides a definite edge to the keeping captains. Butler said, "I think a wicketkeeper has a brilliant view of the game. That can add to your decision-making as you can see first-hand how the wicket is behaving and the way bowlers are bowling"[19]

The IPLs have been a clear fan of the concept with the IPL 2021 having four out of the eight participating teams being captained by wicket-keepers. These included K.L. Rahul for Punjab Kings (2021), Sanju Samson for Rajasthan Royals, MSD for CSK and Rishabh Pant for Delhi Capitals.

Butler further ascribed the growing trend of wicket-keeping captains in the IPL to MSD saying that, "I am sure MSD (Dhoni) has something to do with the sixth sense and breeding of wicketkeepers who can captain. He obviously has been a fantastic captain and there are lots of players who want to follow his footsteps."[19]

19.

Ability to Turn Dark Horses into Game Changer Unicorns

In Indian cricket, there has been a particular cricketer, who was referred to as the dark horse frequently. When he first came into the national side in 2007 everyone knew that he had loads of talent, potential & promise. However, he was raw, brash, an easy starter & impulsive and would very often gift his wicket away after settling down with scores in mid-20s or early 30s by playing a rash shot which would not really be required in the situation. In fact, talent became a nickname cum pejorative for him on media & social media. Then, the magical touch of MSD came who had believed in his potential throughout and kept backing him along with selectors.

MSD asked him to open the innings in early 2013 in the home series against England and he looked solid in that inning, in which he made 80 runs. The move was taken a step further by MSD when he asked him to bat in the ICC's Champions Trophy of 2013, held in England. The move could have backfired as opening the innings in swinging English conditions is usually tricky and requires quick adaptation in one's batting technique to cover it effectively. However, he did not disappoint and made two half-centuries in the tournament by scoring 65 against South Africa and 52 against the West Indies. He never looked back since then, has scored 29 hundreds in his ODI career so far and has been the only IPL captain so far to have won the title 5 times. He is none other than the current captain of the Indian cricket team, i.e., Hitman, Rohit Sharma!

Look at the stark contrast in his batting as an opener vs. as a middle order batsman. As an opener, he has scored 7000+runs in 143 ODI matches with a staggering batting average of 57.44, whereas, his batting average, while batting in the middle order (from no. 4-7), has been a tardy 34.2 in 75 matches played from 2007-2012. However, the important point is that 27 of his 29 ODI career centuries and 3 double-hundreds in ODIs; have all come while opening the innings, with two of his three double hundreds coming within the first 2 years of becoming an opening batsman.

Rohit himself believes that it was a masterstroke which changed the course of his career & life forever. He shared the view in a media interview in early 2017. He said, "I believe the decision to open in

ODIs changed my career and it was a decision taken by MS Dhoni. I became a better batsman after that. In fact it helped me understand my game better, react better according to situations."[20] Rohit further added as to how the decision was communicated to him by MSD in his typical manner, as recounted by the Hitman, "He (Dhoni) just came up to me and said 'I want you to open the innings as I am confident that you will do well. Since you can play both cut and pull shot well, you have the qualities to succeed as an opener'."[20] Rohit further explained, "He told me that I shouldn't be scared of failures or get upset by criticism. He was looking at the bigger picture as the Champions Trophy was scheduled in England that year." [20]

20.

STRONG BELIEF IN MULTI-DIMENSIONAL CAPABILITY – ALL-ROUNDERS

Ravindra Jadeja had a complete transformation under MSD from an underrated, dark horse to a top all-rounder & a virtual game changer with an immense capability to virtually turn the game on its head with the ball, bat or with his fielding. Jadeja said in a recent interview that, 'It has been MSD who carves him to be the best version of him'[21]. He also mentioned about his initial hiccups with shot selection early on in his career and how Dhoni helped him overcome it by advising him, "I remember he said that I was trying to hit shots against balls I shouldn't be attempting."[21] He further added, "Shot selection was something I also felt I was doing wrong. My judgment at the start wasn't right. I would be in double mind. 'Should I go for the shot or no?' These days, I like to take my time and I am clearer in my mind. I know I can always cover up the runs later. That change in thinking has helped."[21]

This is what MSD had to say about Jadeja, way back in Feb 2014 and look at the results he has been delivering with the bat over the recent years. Dhoni said, "It is vital for him to improve as a batsman. He has tremendous potential and the more games he plays, the better he'll get. It isn't about putting too much pressure on him, but it is important that he keeps working on his batting. Once he starts contributing with the bat consistently, we may have a different scenario. We may even look to play with five bowlers outside the subcontinent."[22] That is precisely how it has scripted out for Indian cricket over the recent years with Jadeja becoming an indispensable part of Team India's force structure as a bowling all-rounder capable of contributing immensely with the bat lower down the batting order.

21.

Formation Play – The Arrowhead

Formation play, like formation flying, is when a well-knit team operates & plays in a pre-designated, organized operational structure as per the operating plan. Arrowhead has been one of the most common military formations and is also called the "wedge" formation. As the name suggests, the formation is in the shape or form of an arrow with the tip making it the arrowhead indicating the significance of the tip or the spearhead as the pointman of sorts which makes first contact with the enemy forces. The arrowhead formation is very effective as the maneuvering formation makes direct contact with the enemy with the smallest necessary force while allowing the remaining elements of the formation to maneuver based on the position of the tip or the one in the lead. However, the spearhead or the formation leader does not necessarily have to be at the "tip of the arrowhead". The group leader could be positioned as per situational requirements or based on his ability to lead the formation.

In cricket, this is exactly what MSD has been doing over the years. He has been leading the formation from behind while choosing his arrowhead to take on the enemy forces. Earlier, while leading team India, it was Virat Kohli, who was MSD's spearhead and led the charge for Team India from the front with his bat to chase down huge targets with his determination, grit and masterful stroke-play

with Rohit Sharma and Shikhar Dhawan joining him at the top. Team India, thus, had a top heavy trio with any of them capable of spearheading the inning and taking the attack on to the opposition.

In the IPLs, CSK team, too, operates with the similar top heavy operating doctrine with Ruturaj Gaikwad, Deren Conway, Robin Utthappa and Moeen Ali all capable of launching blitzkrieg against the opposition bowlers on any given day. MSD would simply play the role of formation leader operating quietly from behind the scenes while leading it with a clearly defined limited role for himself usually (on most occasions) as the finisher coming down to bat lower down the order if required.

The formation would normally operate autonomously as per the pre-defined operating plan and team requirements based on conditions and situational requirements on a given day. The formation usually has clearly defined roles and operating modes for every element of it assigned based on each one's unique strengths, capabilities and role in the overall force structure apart from the opposition and operating conditions.

22.

Formation Play – The Elephant Walk

The term 'Elephant Walk' dates back to the World War II era where a large formation of around 1,000 allied bomber aircrafts would usually taxi down the runway and then take off in a single file, in nose-to-tail formations, at minimum interval from each other for bombing missions on enemy positions. Those observed the bombers formation referred to it as Elephant Walk as they looked like elephants walking together on the way to the next watering hole. The Elephant Walk formation is used tactically by the U.S. Air Force (USAF) to practice teamwork and for wartime preparedness of its air squadrons.

How MSD practiced and leveraged the 'Elephant Walk' on the cricket field has been in form of teamwork, wherein, a highly knit, cohesive, high performing, self-directed and motivated team or unit comprising of domain specialists would perform together as a formation with each element of the formation carrying out his assigned role in unison with other elements. Batsman would stick to the overall strategy while batting to their strengths while fully harnessing the wicket and playing conditions while the bowlers would stick to their bowling plans while sticking to their strengths and trying to extract the maximum out of the pitch. Further, every element of the formation usually capable of turning the game on its head as a virtual game changer either with his blitzkrieg with the bat, like

Ruturaj Gaikwad and Robin Uthappa did with their batting onslaught in the powerplay overs in IPL 2021 and 2022 or with a superb bowling performance with the ball to take down the opposition, like Deepak Chahar & Mukesh Choudhary with their swing or Dwayne Bravo with his deception.

When a highly capable & motivated fleet or unit operates in the Elephant Walk mode working in close coordination, tandem & harmony with each other it is highly destructive and it becomes difficult for the opposition to face it as it fully leverages the 'Power of Formation' with the collective sum being always greater than the parts forming it.

23.

Formation Play – The Vertical Charlie

The Vertical Charlie maneuver entails a single fighter jet flying at low altitude pulls up vertically while carrying out rolls and subsequently recovers to its normal attitude. It is also called Upward Roll and very similar to the first half of the Hammerhead maneuver entailing upward, 90-degree climb while performing rolls. How it relates to MSD and the cricket field is how Dhoni comes out to bat in crunch situations, as the savior, required to carry out a difficult rescue operation to take the team out of the danger to safety. He has performed that role in the blue jersey for Team India and in yellow for the CSK on multitude of occasions to the safe zone or to victory with his mighty bat whenever the team required him.

Thus, in the arrowhead, he would lead the team from behind while in the Elephant Walk, he empowers the team to outperform and overwhelm the opposition as a unit and when it all doesn't work out as planned, he would go out on a solo sortie to the middle as the savior for the much required rescue op.

24.

Unleashing the Maverick Side of His Game – Betting on Dark Horses to Win Crunch Situations, Junctures & Games

Greg Chappell, India's one of the most controversial foreign coaches who was at the helm from 2005-2007, when rookie Dhoni was at the peak of his batting prowess, had the following to say about Dhoni, "He had the gambler's streak that set the fine captains apart from the ordinary ones. "He's not reckless. Some of the shots he plays may seem outrageous and risky, but I can assure you he's usually weighed up the options. He knows what he's doing." [23]

He may have been absolutely off the target and wayward with his assessments & analysis on multiple occasions, however, he was bang on target with this one regarding Dhoni. His ability to take calculated risks at crucial junctures of the game paid off well and enabled him to clinch the games from the jaws of potential defeat and the opposition on multiple occasions. He did not do it just with his bat but rather also with his on-field decisions as the captain.

His decision to bowl Joginder Sharma twice, back to back, in the semi final & final of the World Twenty20, has been the hallmark of this abstract theory of his. The decision, however, was not just contrived tactical surprise but in fact was based on Sharma's ability to bowl full and at a pace which was hard for the batsman to hit.

Thus, bringing on rookies, raring to go to the fore at critical junctures of the game, is the real litmus test for any leader. MSD even perfected that art & mastered it with his instinctive approach to the game, honed by him, by practicing & applying it often in real-life, on-field scenarios. However, his unusual calls on the field and strokes with the bat were based on accurate, snap calculations & the fingertip feel anchored in deep experience and powered by one of the finest cricketing brains in the game with almost infinite processing speed & capacity.

25.

Valuing Confidence over Experience

Another key tenet of MSD's leadership playbook has been the ability to bet on promising dark horses and rookies with confidence over experienced campaigners with reluctance. MSD has always valued & embraced confidence, motivation & unconventionality, despite skill limitations and has persisted, while side-stepping embattled rank & credentials battling morale issues, to drive extraordinary results.

He firmly believes that confident & motivated newcomers can be far greater assets and game changers at critical junctures, despite their skill limitations, than well-established players battling confidence and moral issues. That was the reason he gave the ball to Joginder Sharma for bowling the last over as he was raring to go in the final of the ICC's inaugural T20 World Cup of 2007 rather than a reluctant Harbhajan Singh who had an over still left to bowl.

26.

Delegating vs. Directing – Choice of Operating Mode

MSD, as a leader, clearly, has been a patron of Delegating first in the tactical aspects of the game and switching to Directing, if the former seems to be going wayward. However, in the strategic aspects of the game, he has simply been 'Directing' the show. As a captain, he would go for domain specialists, in terms of team selection, and would want them to take their own calls while banking & leveraging their experience especially regarding the tactical bowling plan and field settings.

However, when the plan would not work out, MSD would give the bowler his own plan developed based on a quick assessment of the match's situation, playing conditions and the specific bowler's strengths and weaknesses. However, regarding the overall game plan and the overarching vision, he would hold the cards with himself and direct the show rather than delegating the process to the players.

27.

Balancing Effectively between 'Task' & 'Team'

The leader has to balance the two core aspects of leadership, which are task & people respectively, while running the show and walk the thin tightrope right in the middle, as also outlined by management theorists & authors, Blake & Mouton, in their Managerial Grid or Leadership Grid model, where they also recommend the balancing act, with their Middle-of-the-Road management ideology, of balancing focus on task with concern for people.

However, as per the Managerial Grid, the most effective leadership style is 'Team Management', in which, the leader is passionate about and committed to achieving organizational goals & missions. He inspires, motivates & empowers his team members to work towards achieving the goal while simultaneously also caring & looking after them.

Leaders, however, sometimes tend to err in perfecting this delicate balancing act in their relentless pursuit of operational excellence and going for task focus over people focus leading to disenchantment of team members, internal fissures & conflict and low team morale. However, General Jim Mattis of the U.S. Marine Corps; had a great proscription for leaders on this. He says, on this delicate, balancing act in his advice of caution to leaders, "Do not allow & let your passion for excellence destroy your compassion for thy subordinates."[24]

28.

Keeping the Communication Lines Always Open & Leveraging them Effectively

MSD has always believed in communicating with the team members in a simple, direct and unbiased manner to keep the team morale up and maintaining transparency as a key element of the overall team culture. CSK's opening batsman and seasoned IPL campaigner, Robin Uthappa, revealed the importance placed on team communication by CSK as a team and MS Dhoni himself in a media interview after his advent to CSK from Rajasthan Royals in 2021 which helped him maintain his positive spirit even when he was not in the playing XI.

He said, ""When I came here, that was communicated to me - 'When you get an opportunity, you will get 4 or 5 games for sure. But you have to wait for your opportunity.' For me clarity and communication are very important. So for me, one of thing that I liked about that first conversation with MS was that he told me, 'As of now, you don't walk into my playing XI. We are two months away from IPL. We will see where it goes in the next couple of months. Because I am not thinking about it at this point in time.' Then when I came here, they told me, 'Listen, you are in the top 12 or 13. But you might not get the first game. You might have to wait for your turn.' I said, 'Fair enough, that communication is

there,"[25]

"What was really nice after that was that every week or once in 4-5 days, one coach or the other would come and speak to me and say, 'What can I do for you? How can I help you prepare for what's coming for you? Or, what do you want to improve on?' They understood that, at that point where I played 190 IPL games and I was sitting outside."[25]

29.

Backing the Players 'Fully' & 'Completely'

CSK as a team and MSD as its leader are well renowned for backing its players and giving them long enough window to make them feel secure and prove themselves on the field. One of the most prominent & relevant examples of the same was the IPL 2018, wherein, Shane Watson had not been performing well throughout the tournament. However, the CSK team management kept backing him throughout the season and he ended up scoring a magnificent 100 becoming a game changer in the crucial final of the tournament which made CSK the IPL winner for the third time in 2018.

When asked about the reasons for the incredible success of the CSK as an IPL franchise, Robin Uthappa, the current opening batsman opined, ""I think this is the secret to successful IPL franchises. They have a large support staff. And one of the things as soon as you enter this setup is that there is loyalty and a sense of security within this group. Their trainers and physios have been around since the inception of IPL. And as a player, you see...from the outside, I have seen when CSK give someone an opportunity it is for 5-6 games or even 7 games. They think that you are really good. They bought into you completely as a person and as a player. Like Shane Watson had a bad IPL in 2018 till the finals, right? And then he did something incredible for us. Similar with Sureshy (Suresh Raina) as well. There are times when he

wouldn't have performed well in the first 8 games. But they have stuck with him and suddenly, in the last 6 games, he has changed the whole course of the tournament with his performances," he said.[25]

Shane Watson himself thanked coach Stephen Fleming and skipper MSD for the same in an interview,he said, "That you go 10 games without scoring runs and still get picked (laughs). Last season, thank you MS Dhoni and Stephen Fleming for keeping the faith. That was phenomenal and made me feel that good to go, a bit a block would not stop me."[26]

30. Inclusive Approach even for CSK Players Not in the Playing XI

Another reason for CSK's successes and MSD's leadership has been the inclusive approach even for players who are not in the playing XI which boosts the dug-out's morale tremendously and keeps the spirits up. Robin Uthappa mentioned the same in one of his recent interviews referring to his own experience, "It was very easy for someone who has played those many matches to become negative. But what helped me keep that good attitude was that they spoke to me and made sure I was paid attention to at practice when the main guys who were in the XI weren't practicing. I truly believe that the health of a good IPL team or a successful IPL team is very reliant on how the guys who are not in the XI are taken care off because they set the atmosphere and the tone of the team."[25]

MSD did the same in IPL 2020 when he thanked the CSK players who were not part of the playing XI in a post match presentation after one of the games for keeping the chins up and overall spirit high contributing to the overall team morale & motivation.

31.

Keeping Things Simple and Making Even Complex Things Simple

MS Dhoni has this knack of keeping things simple rather than getting bogged down by complex jargons or complex thinking process. He prefers to keep things simple, in his life as well as game and when surrounded by complexity he breaks things down into simple chunks. Even in his communication with the team, he emphasizes to keep things simple as he does not want to complicate things as he believes complexity creates confusion for the team.

He himself said in one his interviews, "What works for me is to keep things simple in life. Cricket is a simple sport: You see the ball, you hit the ball. But you can make it complex: is it an inswing or an outswing, is it a yorker or a bouncer? You can keep on adding layers of complexity to the game and this applies to your life too. But if you are honest to yourself, you will take good decisions."[27]

Even Shane Watson , former CSK opener mentioned the same about him in an interview. He said, "Sitting on a plain and there is a TV screen in front of me showing documentary on MS. I remember watching his documentary and I did not know the extent of the

impact he has on Indian cricket and especially Indian public in general. When he has his long hair and then he cut it off, around about that time. The thing that stands out to me, after getting to know him in the last 3 years is how easily he simplifies a complex situation,"[26]

32.

Staying Calm under Pressure

One of the most remarkable abilities of MSD has been his ability to remain calm and ice cool under pressure. When asked about this ability of his, he replied, "Being prepared will always keep you cool. Whether you are a student or a pro athlete you have to get into the zone. The zone is a state of performing with zero friction. Practice and preparation will always help you perfect your skills and get you in the zone. If your skills go up, stress goes down. Psychologists say that 10,000 hours of practice will always get you to your goal!"[27]

His stoic demeanor makes him non-expressive especially when it comes to his emotions even when he is feeling them deep inside. Further, he believes in putting logic over emotion and thus keeps his head cool at all times while not letting himself be swayed by the moment and the flow of emotions. That enables him to stay in the moment and keep thinking off his feet about the best tactical plan to manage the situation in the best possible manner, be it bowler selection, bowling plan by the bowlers, field setting, creating set-pieces, making the best plan based on batsmen, bowling options available and their comparative strengths & relevance to match situation etc.

Former Indian Captain, Sourav Ganguly ratified the same in a media interview, "MS has this fantastic ability to remain calm under any situation. Lot of people have asked me that "you have been with him, so how does he remain calm? I tell them that he doesn't show it. From inside he is different, from outside he is different. That goes around in the dressing room and he gets a lot of respect. We only look at the criticism but amount of respect he gets in India is unbelievable," [28]

33.

Focus on the Process Rather than Results or Outcomes

The most important, simple and critical piece of advice that has come from the legend over the years has been to just focus on the process rather than results as when we start focusing on the outcomes the process goes haywire as we tend to play under the pressure of outcomes and when we play fearlessly, giving our best and without bothering about the outcome the results take care of themselves. MSD has done it over and over again and the triple crown of cricket won by Team India under him bears testimony to that!

34. "Great Captains Make Players Believe in Themselves When They Have Lost It"

On the 15th Anniversary of India's unforgettable win in the T20 World Cup 2007, Sreesanth, the man with golden hands which took India across the line with the winning catch had the following to say about MSD in an interview given to NDTV earlier today. He said while praising Dhoni's captaincy: "Best captains work with individuals and believe in the players. And even when the players don't believe in themselves, the great captains will come up to you and make you believe in your belief system"[29].

Decrypting Dhoni's decision to give the ball to Joginder Sharma for the last over, he revealed, "We all have played together for Indan Airlines in the forming years. So Dhoni bhai knows Jogi bhai's winning attitude. And he knows Jogi bhai has done it not just once and twice, he has done it many times. He had a lot of faith in him"[29].

35.

Creating that 'Special Connect' with the Players

After the round 2 of the series of India-Pakistan nail-biters in the Asia Cup, Virat Kohli elaborated in the post match presentation as to how MSD was the only one who messaged him to buck him up when King Kohli left test captaincy earlier in Jan 2022 at the peak of his game and nobody else bothered. Dhoni-Kohli chemistry is almost fabled and their on-field partnerships with the bat scripted multiple wins for Team India over the years gone by with the duo sharing great camaraderie and a very special bond of mutual respect and appreciation going way above and beyond the formal captain-vice captain hierarchical roles with MSD having effectively groomed and shaped Kohli's growth and rise as the leader.

Thus, when Kohli called it quits as the leader and hung up his captain's arm band, MSD was the one to connect despite of it not being required formally. That's an extraordinary and special leader who stays connected to his select comrades & troops at the human level during their life's personal ups and downs even after having left command and the uniform... That's the human connect & touch and that's what separates great leaders from just leaders!

36.

The 'Calming Influence' - On the Team & the Players

Hardik Pandya, the self-confessed MSD acolyte and disciple, has proved to be critical for Team India with once again playing a critical role in the unmatched clash of the Asian giants with India getting the better of arch-rival Pakistan in Dubai in their opening encounter of the Asia Cup 2022.

Hardik bowled superbly getting 3 wickets and batted in characteristic MSD style while chasing under pressure to take India across the finish line in the last over. His non-chalant demeanour and absolute calmness in holding the nerve amid the high voltage India-Pak rivalry had clear shades and streaks of the original master & legend of the finishing game, MSD, and Hardik's inning simply brought the memories of MSD's on-field heroics alive!

He himself said in the post match presentation that staying calm under pressure is something he learnt from Dhoni as an invaluable trait and it makes him assess and respond to situations better while navigating his course to the finish line. Hardik in a conversation with ESPN CricInfo elaborated

as to how MSD influenced and shaped his thinking, temperament with the infusion of calmness and approach to the game as a mentor, guru and elder bro.

37. Honesty with Self and in Life

Two words which quintessentially capture the essence of MSD's persona and his leadership are 'honesty' and 'humility' which have shaped, led and guided his personal as well as professional life forever and have enabled him to achieve what he has truly deserved - honour, respect & unflinching loyalty of his teammates as the extraordinary leader and, of course, the triple crown of cricket. How honesty helps someone is that it enables one to face and accept the harsh reality, including, setbacks, skill limitations, shortcomings etc. the way it is. And when one accepts the reality it starts the chain reaction of change, improvement and betterment. As per the venerable Kübler-Ross model of change, a person goes through the following five stages when faced with an emotional setback or undesired change:- Denial, Anger, Bargaining, Depression and Acceptance. If, being honest to ourselves, we straightway 'accept' the reality the way it is by somehow managing to bypass the emotional clouds and start from there, it really shortens the curve. That's what Dhoni, being his stoic self, does very effectively always which takes him really ahead of his current reality really quickly in the future-focused mode. Also, a person can really be honest and fair with others only if he is honest with himself with a strong moral compass and that's why it becomes indispensable to success in the leadership role... So, the proverbial wisdom, 'honesty is the best policy' indeed still holds...Q.E.D. by MSD!

38.

The Power of Belief

MS Dhoni is well known for fully backing his players and believing in them which, in turn, makes them believe in themselves and their capabilities even more and brings out the best in them on the field. That's not just limited to Indian players but even international players have lauded this ability of MSD as the leader of the pack. When Ngidi came to India to play his first IPL season for CSK in 2018, he has mentioned as to how he felt reassured and confident when a cricketer of 'MSD's class and calibre' showed his faith in him and how it inspired him and made him do well in front of thousands of spectators in fully packed Indian stadiums which was completely unusual for him. Deepak Chahar, the spearhead of CSK's pace bowling battery, also has elaborated as to how playing for CSK and MSD's faith drove his personal transformation from being a fringe bowler at the outset to being the 'king of swing' and a top of the line powerplay specialist bowler which effectively turned his career around.

That's the power of faith and belief which turns even an ordinary man into a virtual Superman! When the leader believes in and backs his team to the hilt and inspires them to give all that they have got, the results are simply extraordinary...

39.

"When Everyone was Critical, Dhoni Backed Me" - Bravo - Having Faith in and Backing the Players Fully

MSD has this special quality of believing in and fully backing the players he chooses for his playing XI and thereafter he sticks to them giving each individual ample opportunities to express themselves on the field freely without the pressure of expectations or fear of getting benched. The same has been corroborated by many players over the years.

Shane Watson did not do well with the bat throughout IPL 2018 but Dhoni kept backing him unflinchingly and Watson ultimately played a magnificent century, a match winning knock against SRH in the final to let CSK lay their hands on the coveted trophy for the third time after a long hiatus. Ngidi, too, recently mentioned as to how being backed by a player of Dhoni's caliber and class helped him do well in his first IPL season in 2018.

Dwayne Bravo outlined as to how when everyone was critical of him and his bowling in IPL 2018, Dhoni kept backing him fully and that made him really do well. When the leader keeps believing in his team and backs them fully despite the performances and outcomes, it reassures and instills the self-belief back in them, especially, the players going through a rough patch and it really works like magic. Ask MSD disciples and acolytes who have witnessed it firsthand!

40.

Being the 'Leader' even without being the 'Captain'

MSD played as a player rather than as the captain of CSK during the first half of IPL 2022 with Jaddu being the skipper. Prior to this, MSD also played in the blue jersey under Virat Kohli's captaincy from early 2017 till the ICC's ODI World Cup in 2019. However, both the times it was actually about MSD and how he led the team from behind as the 'Chacha Chaudhary' with his extraordinary domain competence and brilliant situational leadership.

But how does MSD manage to be the undisputed leader of the outfit even when he is not the designated captain. Simply, with the honor and respect he deservingly gets from his troops as the natural leader and an absolute authority on the game with his uncannily accurate Fingerspitzengefühl, brilliant reading of the game and natural talent for conducting real time, on-field mentorship of players and viewers (via stump mic) from behind the stumps...

BIBLIOGRAPHY

1. "IPL 2020: MS Dhoni Admits He Was Not Able To Middle Lot Of Deliveries As CSK Suffer Third Straight Defeat", PTI, October 03, 2020

   https://www.outlookindia.com/website/story/sports-news-ipl-2020-ms-dhoni-admits-he-was-not-able-to-middle-lot-of-deliveries-as-csk-suffer-third-straight-defeat/361396

2. "MS Dhoni delays return to Ranchi till all his CSK teammates depart", Indian Express, Devendra Pandey, May 08, 2021

   https://indianexpress.com/article/sports/ipl/ms-dhoni-delays-return-to-ranchi-till-all-his-csk-teammates-depart-7303778/

3. "TOI Exclusive: Virat Kohli and Ravi Shastri on World Cup, MS Dhoni, Bumrah and More", The Times of India, May 15, 2019, By K Shriniwas Rao,

   https://timesofindia.indiatimes.com/sports/cricket/icc-world-cup/icc-world-cup-2019-god-filters-everyone-says-virat-kohli/articleshow/69334767.cms

4. IPL 2022: Not "End of the World" if CSK don't make playoffs, says MS Dhoni https://sports.ndtv.com/ipl-2022/ipl-2022-not-end-of-the-world-if-csk-dont-make-playoffs-says-ms-dhoni-2957996

5. "What is charisma? Body Language Quick Takes #9",
Forbes, By Nick Morgan, Oct 06, 2011
https://www.forbes.com/sites/nickmorgan/2011/10/06/wh
at-is-charisma-body-language-quick-takes-
9/?sh=3380ab4e130f

6. "The Most Charismatic General Ever?" Forbes, By Nick
Morgan, June 20, 2013
https://www.forbes.com/sites/nickmorgan/2013/06/20/th
e-most-charismatic-general-ever/?sh=64dc4c7e4389

7. Scouller, J. (2011). The Three Levels of Leadership: How to
Develop Your Leadership Presence, Knowhow and Skill.
Cirencester: Management Books 2000., ISBN 9781852526818

8. "I would go to war with Dhoni by my side: Gary Kirsten",
DNA India, By Vijay Tagore, June 18, 2011,
https://www.dnaindia.com/sports/report-i-would-go-to-
war-with-dhoni-by-my-side-gary-kirsten-1556275

9. "If there's commitment, that's victory for me", ESPN
Cricinfo, March 24, 2008, By Siddhartha Vaidyanathan and
Nagraj Gollapudi https://www.espncricinfo.com/story/if-
there-s-commitment-that-s-victory-for-me-343750

10. "MS Dhoni lauds Mukesh Choudhary, Simarjeet Singh for
Outstanding Bowling Spell vs. MI", Republic World, May 13,
2022 https://www.republicworld.com/sports-news/ipl-
2022/ms-dhoni-lauds-mukesh-choudhary-simarjeet-singh-
for-outstanding-spell-bowling-vs-mi-articleshow.html

11. IPL 2022 | Mukesh Choudhary was at his best with new ball, says Aakash Chopra, Sportscafe June 08, 2022 https://sportscafe.in/cricket/articles/2022/jun/08/ipl-2022-mukesh-choudhary-was-at-his-best-with-new-ball-says-aakash-chopra

12. "How MS Dhoni inspired Mukesh Choudhary to bowl the final over against SRH", Sportslump, https://sportslumo.com/ipl-2022/ipl-2022-srh-vs-cs-how-ms-dhoni-inspired-mukesh-choudhary-to-bowl-the-final-over-against-srh/

13. "Mukesh Choudhary reveals what MS Dhoni told him during the last over against SRH", ANI May 02, 2022 https://www.aninews.in/news/sports/cricket/ipl-2022-mukesh-choudhary-reveals-what-ms-dhoni-told-him-during-last-over-against-srh20220502105116/

14. MS Dhoni Talks about Art of Leadership, India Times, July 08, 2014, https://www.indiatimes.com/sports/cricket/ms-dhoni-my-gut-feeling-is-driven-by-experience-logic-159979.html

15. Burns, J.M, (1978), Leadership, N.Y, Harper and Row

16. Bass, B. M,(1985), Leadership and Performance, N.Y. Free Press

17. "MS Dhoni's Wicket-Keeping Style Should Not be Aped by Youngsters: Syed Kirmani", Outlook Magazine, Outlook Web Bureau, October 09, 2018 https://www.outlookindia.com/website/story/ms-dhonis-

wicket-keeping-style-should-not-be-aped-by-youngsters-syed-kirmani/318018

18. "TOI Exclusive: Virat Kohli and Ravi Shastri on World Cup, MS Dhoni, Bumrah and More", The Times of India, May 15, 2019, By K Shriniwas Rao, https://timesofindia.indiatimes.com/sports/cricket/icc-world-cup/icc-world-cup-2019-god-filters-everyone-says-virat-kohli/articleshow/69334767.cms

19. 'MSD, the inspiration behind keeper-captains', The Hindu, PTI, April 11, 2021 https://www.thehindu.com/sport/cricket/msd-the-inspiration-behind-keeper-captains/article34297121.ece

20. "Rohit Sharma reveals how MS Dhoni helped transform his career", NDTV Sports Eng, January 11, 2017, Edited by Dattaraj Thaly https://sports.ndtv.com/cricket/rohit-sharma-reveals-how-ms-dhoni-helped-transform-his-career-1647710

21. "Jadeja Names Dhoni as the Key Person for his Transformation", Times of Sports, June 01, 2021 https://www.timesofsports.com/cricket/news/jadeja-praises-dhoni/

22. "How Ravindra Jadeja made the leap", HT Mint, By Chetan Narula, Feb 05, 2014

https://www.livemint.com/Leisure/BrUjVnQm8pZNw3HS
su6UEO/How-Ravindra-Jadeja-made-the-leap.html

23. "Grace under fire", ESPN CricInfo, By Dileep
Premachandran, Sep 26, 2007
https://www.espncricinfo.com/story/top-performer-
mahendra-singh-dhoni-312575

24. "Jim Mattis once pulled Christmas duty for a young Marine –
and it's the perfect holiday story", CNBC make it, By Vanna
Le, https://www.cnbc.com/2018/12/21/why-jim-mattis-
once-pulled-christmas-duty-for-a-young-marine.html

25. "In first conversation with Dhoni he said, 'You don't walk
into my XI": IPL veteran on what makes CSK 'successful'",
HT Sports Desk, Hindustan Times, April 10, 2022
https://www.hindustantimes.com/cricket/in-first-
conversation-with-ms-dhoni-he-said-you-don-t-walk-into-my-
xi-india-batter-robin-uthappa-reveals-key-to-csk-s-ipl-success-
101649509439316.html

26. IPL 2020: Retired CSK batsman Shane Watson thanks MS
Dhoni for not dropping him despite bad performances
https://www.indiatoday.in/sports/ipl-2020/story/shane-
watson-retires-thanks-ms-dhoni-not-dropping-him-10-
innings-without-scoring-documentary-billion-people-in-
chennai-fans-1737947-2020-11-04

27. "Captain Cool: 8 Questions with Mahendra Singh Dhoni",
braingainmag.com, Uttara Choudhary, October 03, 2016

https://www.braingainmag.com/captain-cool-eight-questions-with-mahendra-singh-dhoni.htm

28. "Mahendra Singh Dhoni Has 'Fantastic' Ability to Stay Calm Under Pressure: Sourav Ganguly", NDTV Sports, February 04, 2016 https://sports.ndtv.com/cricket/mahendra-singh-dhoni-has-fantastic-ability-to-stay-calm-under-pressure-sourav-ganguly-1487444

29. "He Knew Jogi Bhai's Winning Attitude" Sreesanth on Why M.S. Dhoni", News18.com https://www.news18.com/cricketnext/news/he-knew-jogi-bhais-winning-attitude-sreesanth-on-why-ms-dhoni-handed-joginder-sharma-the-hostoric-final-over-6031897.html

ABOUT THE AUTHOR

Rajat Narang is the Co-Founder and Partner of a niche Research Firm pivoted on the Global Aerospace & Defense Industry for over a decade now apart from being a serial Author and active Podcaster.

He has authored over 2000+ syndicated research reports (across industries & sectors) and has authored around 8 books on Commercial & Military Aviation and Leadership. The end users of his reports have been senior executives of leading Commercial & Military Aviation OEMs led by Airbus, Boeing, Bombardier, Embraer, Gulfstream, Dassault, Textron Aviation and their supplier base, including, engine OEMs and T1 suppliers such as GE Aviation, Rolls Royce, Pratt & Whitney, Safran & Spirit Aerosystems. His reports have also been leveraged by the U.S. Air Force, Lockheed Martin Corporation, BAE Systems, General Dynamics Land Systems and Korean Aerospace Industries (KAI) on the defense side of A&D.

His educational background includes a Masters in Business Administration (MBA) in International Business from the Indian

Institute of Foreign Trade (IIFT) with Business Strategy as the core pivot followed by a Masters in Political Science with specialization in International Relations.

His podcasts, "Birds of Fray: Top Gun Maverick" and "M.S. Dhoni: Leadership Masterclass from the Master of the Craft" are available on most leading global platforms, including, Amazon Music, Spotify, Audible, Apple Podcasts & Google Podcasts and have a substantial following.

Bitten early by the A&D, Strategy & Leadership bugs while growing up, he has been actively following, tracking & pursuing them for almost 2 decades now.